LOST MAGIC
THE VERY BEST OF
BRIAN MOSES

LOST MAGIC

THE VERY BEST OF

BRIAN MOSES

ILLUSTRATED
BY
CHRIS GARBUTT

MACMILLAN CHILDREN'S BOOKS

First published 2016 by Macmillan Children's Books
an imprint of Pan Macmillan
20 New Wharf Road, London N1 9RR
Associated companies throughout the world
www.panmacmillan.com

ISBN 978-1-5098-3874-5

1 3 5 7 9 8 6 4 2

A CIP catalogue record for this book is available from
the British Library.

Printed and bound by CPI Group (UK) Ltd, Croydon CR0 4YY

This one has to be for the three ladies in my life:
My wife Anne, and my daughters Karen & Linette.

CONTENTS

CLOSER TO HOME . . .

I DON'T WANT TO BELIEVE WHAT I'M TOLD . . .

IN ALL THESE LIVES I'VE LIVED BEFORE . . .

IMPROBABLE OR IMPOSSIBLE?

I NEVER EXPECTED FIREFLIES . . .

ONCE UPON A TIME THERE WERE UNICORNS . . .

HOW COOL IS SCHOOL?

THE DEAD DON'T TELL TALES, OR DO THEY?

PARENTS, WHO NEEDS THEM?

EYES, WINGS, DRAGON FLAME . . .

A WATERFALL OF POSSIBILITIES . . .

INTRODUCTION

A question I'm asked at almost every poetry performance for children is, 'What's your favourite poem?'

I find it impossible to answer. Would it be a poem that always seems to go down well in a performance, or a poem that means something special to me, or a recent poem that I'm excited about? I just don't know.

So in this book, and with the help of Gaby Morgan, who has been my editor at Macmillan since 1993, I've collected together one hundred or so poems that might be contenders for the label 'My favourite poem'.

Included are poems that I'm always being asked to read – 'The Sssssnake Hotel', 'Billy's Coming Back', 'Shopping Trolley', 'What Teachers Wear in Bed' and 'Walking with My Iguana'. These are what I call 'performance poems', and I often accompany their reading with percussion instruments to underpin the rhythms.

Then there are poems that I hope are more thoughtful, because poetry shouldn't just make us smile or laugh – it should make us think and wonder; it should make us feel sad or frightened. Poetry touches every emotion. I couldn't think of putting together a 'Best of' selection without including poems such as 'A Feather from an Angel', 'Lost Magic', 'Playing with Stars', 'White Horse', 'Days' or 'Space Dog'.

Then there are some new poems too, that may well

become favourites as time passes. But as to which of my poems could be my all-time favourite, I just don't know.

Really I'm much keener to find out what *your* favourite poem is.

What I do know is that each poem here points to a particular time in my life, and I remember where most of them were written and what inspired them.

They are all signposts along the road that I've travelled since 1988 when I became a professional writer.

I hope you enjoy the collection as much as I enjoyed compiling it.

Brian Moses

A FEATHER FROM AN ANGEL

Anton's box of treasures held
a silver key and a glassy stone,
a figurine made of polished bone
and a feather from an angel.

The figurine was from Borneo,
the stone from France or Italy,
the silver key was a mystery
but the feather came from an angel.

We might have believed him if he'd said
the feather fell from a bleached white crow
but he always replied, 'It's an angel's, I know,
a feather from an angel.'

We might have believed him if he'd said,
'An albatross let the feather fall,'
But he had no doubt, no doubt at all,
his feather came from an angel.

'I thought I'd dreamt him one night,' he'd say,
'But in the morning I knew he'd been there;
he left a feather on my bedside chair,
a feather from an angel.'

And it seems that all my life I've looked
for that sort of belief that nothing could shift,
something simple yet precious as Anton's gift,
a feather from an angel.

AN INDIAN
PYTHON
WILL WELCOME
YOU . . .

THE SSSSNAKE HOTEL

An Indian python will welcome you
to the Ssssnake hotel.
As he finds your keys he'll maybe enquire
if you're feeling well.
And he'll say that he hopes you survive the night,
that you sleep without screaming
and don't die of fright
at the Ssssnake hotel.

There's an anaconda that likes to wander
the corridors at night,
and a boa that will lower itself on to guests
as they search for the light.
And if, by chance, you lie awake
and nearby something hisses,
I warn you now, you're about to be covered
with tiny vipery kisses,
at the Ssssnake hotel.

And should you hear a chorus of groans
coming from the room next door,
and the python cracking someone's bones,
please don't go out and explore.
Just ignore all the screams
and the strangled yells
when you spend a weekend
at the Ssssnake hotel.

GOING SOUTH

Word gets round
by word of mouth
or word of beak,
'We're going south.'

And everyone gathers
on telephone wires,
on tops of trees
on roofs or church spires.

No security checks,
no passport, no cases.
No border controls
closing off places.

The skies are ours,
we go where we please,
away from the damp
and the winter freeze.

And even though
they've only just come,
a party of swifts
on runway number one

are given priority
so everyone waits
while there's last minute preening
or chatting with mates

till the skyway clears
and it's time to go,
'See you in Spain,'
'Meet you in Rio.'

We went there last year,
we know where we're going,
stretch out, lift off,
feel the air flowing.

Over the mountains,
the buildings and trees,
we're going south
on the pull of the breeze.

WALKING DOGS, CHRISTMAS DAY
(Yorkshire Moors, 2009)

One dog guides us through the fields
on a route she's followed for years.
No matter the track has disappeared
under layers of snow, Old-timer Charlie
still knows which way to go.

Fern just wants to play, to bullet herself
through drifting snow. Six months old,
she's never seen the fields white out
like this before. Suddenly her world becomes
a wet and wacky playground she can't ignore.

Lucy wants to confide in us.
She knows this place, has seen it change,
summer gold to winter white.
She holds us spellbound, hints at secrets
only dogs discover, closer to the ground.

Bruno cracks us up, part dachshund
part terrier, long narrow face
like Uncle Bulgaria, barely bigger
than the depth of snow, squeezes his shape,
cartoon-like, into spaces he shouldn't go.

But Scampi stays at home, snug in her own
small hiding hole. Nothing we say
can persuade her to come, the snow too deep,
the ice too cold. She'll hibernate
till old bones feel a warmer season unfold.

MISSING - GREY-AND-WHITE CAT, ANSWERS TO THE NAME OF FREDDY

Why is it
I find it hard to believe
that Freddy will come
when you call?
Even if you threw open your windows
and bawled out his name,
not once, not twice,
but for a full fifteen minutes
of neighbourhood fame,
I just don't think that Freddy
will answer.

Cats roam, we know.
Cats find a welcoming mat
on the sunnier side of the road.
He'll have his paws
tucked under someone else's table
by now.
Or maybe he's eloped
with some cat he duetted with
on the corner one night.
Maybe she turned his head,
poor Fred, he's hooked by now,
couldn't come back
if he wanted to.

So it's no good
you putting up posters
all over Camden Town
for even if you bawl and yell
each night for a week,
you may find an Eddie
or even a Teddy
trying your cat flap for size.

But whatever answers
won't be Freddy.
You can bet nine lives
that Freddy's gone
till he's ready
to stroll back home.

WALKING WITH MY IGUANA

(Words in brackets to be replaced by another voice or voices)

I'm walking (I'm walking)
with my iguana (with my iguana)

I'm walking (I'm walking)
with my iguana (with my iguana)

When the temperature rises
to above eighty-five,
my iguana is looking
like he's coming alive.

So we make it to the beach,
my iguana and me,
then he sits on my shoulder
as we stroll by the sea . . .

and I'm walking (I'm walking)
with my iguana (with my iguana)

I'm walking (I'm walking)
with my iguana (with my iguana)

Well if anyone sees us
we're a big surprise,
my iguana and me
on our daily exercise,

11

till somebody phones
the local police
and says I have an alligator
tied to a leash

when I'm walking (I'm walking)
with my iguana (with my iguana)

I'm walking (I'm walking)
with my iguana (with my iguana)

It's the spines on his back
that make him look grim,
but he just loves to be tickled
under his chin.

And my iguana will tell me
that he's ready for bed
when he puts on his pyjamas
and lays down his sleepy (Yawn) head.

And I'm walking (I'm walking)
with my iguana (with my iguana)

still walking (still walking)
With my iguana (with my iguana)

with my iguana . . .

with my iguana . . .

and my piranha

and my chihuahua

and my chinchilla,

with my groovy gorilla

my caterpillar . . .

and I'm walking . . .

with my iguana . . . . . .

ELEPHANTS CAN'T JUMP

Elephants can't jump, and that's a fact.
So it's no good expecting an elephant to jump for joy
if you tell him some good news.
You won't make an elephant jump
if you sound a loud noise behind him –
elephants can't jump.
You won't see an elephant skipping or pole-vaulting.
It wasn't an elephant that jumped over the moon
when the little dog laughed,
and contrary to popular belief
elephants do not jump when they see mice.
Elephants, with their great bulk,
don't like to leave the ground.
Elephants and jumping do not go well together.

And perhaps it's all for the best,
for if elephants did jump, just think
of all the trouble they'd cause.
If all the elephants in Africa linked trunks
and jumped together,
their combined weight on landing
would cause a crack in the Earth's crust.
Just think if elephants were jumping for joy
every time they won the lottery
or welcomed baby elephants into the world,
they'd probably have a knock-on effect
and all the rest of us would shoot skywards
when they landed.

I'm rather pleased to discover that elephants can't jump . . .
The world suddenly seems that tiny bit safer.

TAKING OUT THE TIGERS

At twilight time
or early morning
a tiger-sized ROAR
is a fearsome warning
as a huge cat swaggers
through a fine sea mist,
its paws the size
of a boxer's fist,

when they're
taking out the tigers
on Sandown beach.

These tough kitties
have something to teach
about the law of the jungle
on Sandown beach.
And any kind of dog
would be most unwise
to challenge a cat
that's this sort of size,

when they're
taking out the tigers
on Sandown beach.

As a weak sun sinks
in a winter sky,

it reflects in the jewel
of a tiger's eye,
but an Indian Ocean
is dreams away
from the chilly surf
of Sandown Bay,

when they're
taking out the tigers
on Sandown beach,
taking out the tigers
on Sandown Beach,
taking out the
tigerrrrrrrrrrrs.

(They really did walk the tigers from Sandown Zoo along the beach in winter.)

FOUR-SECOND MEMORY

Is it a fact or is it a hype
that a goldfish suffers a memory wipe
every time four seconds passes by
and if it's true, does he wonder why?
Perhaps that's why he's happy to swim
round and round in his tank, nothing bothers him.
Four seconds and then his mind is wiped clean,
four seconds and he's no idea where he's been.
So every circuit's a different view,
every circuit brings something new.
Does he ever get feelings of 'deja-vu'
or say to another fish, 'Don't I know you?
Haven't we met some place before?'
But after four seconds the slam of a door
erases the thought from his memory bank
and he'll take another tour of his tank.

In a goldfish world there could never be
any sense of goldfish history.
They could never follow serials on TV,
their lives must be one big mystery –
What did I do, what have I seen,
who did I meet, where have I been?
Do they suffer four seconds of stress?
Could one ever be called as a witness?
'Where were you on the night of the crime?'
He'd really have no notion of time.
Adrift in the water, he's floating and flowing
with only four seconds to know where he's going.
Four seconds and then his mind is wiped clean
and the goldfish has no idea where he's been.

AT THE ZOO

If you want to get married at London Zoo
this is what we can offer you . . .

A four metre long reticulated snake
gift-wrapped round your wedding cake.
A choir of hyenas singing loud,
a congregation of apes from rent-a-crowd.
Two charming chimps that will bridesmaid you
and if you need a witness use a kangaroo
at the zoo, at the zoo, at the zoo.

The waiters look great in their penguin suits,
the monkeys will serve you selected fruits.
The alligators are simply delighted,
even ocelots get quite excited.
The Vietnamese pot bellied pigs
will take to their toes and dance wedding jigs.
at the zoo, at the zoo, at the zoo.

The lions look forward to welcoming you
to your wedding breakfast here at the zoo,
and any leftovers they'd be pleased to chew
at the zoo, at the zoo, at the zoo.

Yes, we look forward to marrying you
at the zoo, at the zoo, at the zoo.

THE DINOSAUR NEXT DOOR

I'm in love with the dinosaur next door,
she's a really fabulous creature with an operatic ROAR.
She's the loveliest, most talented dinosaur on our street
and she shimmers like a diamond on a pair of sparkling
      feet.

Yes, I'm in love with the dinosaur next door
but our love must be a secret, something we must both
      ignore.
For she's already married to a sharp tooth carnivore
who is handy with his muscles, but she thinks him quite
      a bore.

He really isn't known for his charm and sensitivity,
in fact his speciality's a certain proclivity
to first rip you to shreds and then ask questions later,
in fact he would be perfect as an armoured gladiator.

So we take romantic walks, my dinosaur and I,
and I hold her claw in mine as we watch the world pass by
while I tell her she should leave him and spend her life
      with me
but she's frightened that he'd kill me if ever she'd agree.

So I spend my time alone, mostly in misery,
as I think about my dinosaur and what isn't meant to be.
My future looks cold and bleak since she's stolen my heart
and like Romeo and Juliet we're doomed to be apart.

WHATEVER NEXT T. REX?

*(The theropod dinosaurs, like Tyrannosaurus Rex
and Velociraptor, were some of the most fearsome
carnivores ever. Yet some scientists say that most of
these perfect hunters abandoned live prey in favour of
a more peaceful, vegetarian existence. . . which started
their evolution into birds.)*

I don't know what to believe any more,
I don't know what to think.
Latest scientific theories
have caused a bit of a stink!
It feels like someone's pulled the carpet
out from under our feet
now that scientists are telling us
T. Rexes stopped eating meat!

I just don't know, I can't believe
this can possibly be right.
This creature who stalked our nightmares
and gave us all a fright,
suddenly became meek and gentle,
a lapdog of a beast,
who came home each night, kissed his wife
and sat down to his veggie feast!

They reckon he ate nut cutlets
instead of dinosaur steak,
and the reason he roared so much
was probably bellyache.

They'd have us believe Tyrannosaurus
was a pillar of society,
that his public image is wrong
and he didn't deserve such notoriety.

He used to be the most macho creature
that ever walked the Earth.
In any dinosaur football team
who knows what he'd have been worth?
This wonderful striker of terror
into the hearts of opposing teams,
this superhero of Prehistoric movies,
sleek, savage killing machine.

And it's funny how things fall apart
when you least expect them to,
a certainty I've trusted for years
now possibly untrue.
And I always believed what I heard
from scientists and librarians,
but now they tell me it's likely
T. Rexes became vegetarians!

RETURN TO THE
SSSSNAKE HOTEL

If it's thrills that you're after
It's thrills that you'll get,
when you enter the foyer
to find that you're met
by a python who's eyeing you up
as a snack,
and the mambas, all dressed
for dinner in black,
as they smile deadly smiles
to welcome you back
to the snake, to the snake,
to the ssssnake hotel.

Had you really forgotten
that last time you stayed,
the deadly death rattle
that the rattlesnakes made,
and that dip in the pool
with a water snake,
how that nearly became
a fatal mistake
at the snake, at the snake,
at the ssssnake hotel.

But now that you're back
won't you chance a dance
with a sweetly poisonous
fer de lance,
or relax in the lounge
playing snakes and ladders
with one or two
competitive adders
at the snake, at the snake,
at the ssssnake hotel.

So tonight, if a viper
slips into your room,
or a cobra dances
to some non-existent tune,
we'll give you some vouchers
to our sister hotel,
(where tarantulas spin their webs
round your feet
and black widows search
for husbands to eat,)
at the spider, the spider,
the sssspider motel.

WHAT DO YOU DO NOW YOU'VE BEEN TO THE MOON?

ROCKET-WATCHING PARTY

*(Jaycee Beach was the nearest beach to Cape
Canaveral – later renamed Cape Kennedy – where
rockets were launched. In the 1950s there were regular
rocket-watching parties along the beach.)*

There's a rocket-watching party
at the beach tonight
and we'll cheer the rocket
till it's way out of sight.

Bring something to eat,
bring burgers and Coke
bring binoculars
for the first sign of smoke.

We'll pick up driftwood
from along the shore,
build up a fire
as we wait for the roar,

for the whoosh of flame
that grows higher and higher
reaching to the heavens
in a trail of fire.

And we'll tremble from excitement
or maybe fear
as it blusters skywards
then disappears.

And all of us want to be
rocket engineers,
pilots or scientists,
space pioneers.

But sometimes we wait
and we wait and wait
and nothing happens
and it's getting late.

Till a message comes through,
no launch tonight.
Countdown's called off
it just didn't go right.

Then it's just another night
on Jaycee Beach
when the stars still seem
so far out of reach.

SPACE DOG

She must have been someone's pet,
sometime before the scientists
found her, tagged and labelled her
suitable for space.
She had, someone said,
a trusting face.

She must have been shocked
when the ones she'd trusted
strapped her down
in some strange contraption,
stroked her head, tickled
under her chin, then left,
and locked her in.

She must have been cowed
by the rocket's power,
shaken by the roar, the thrust
must have left her
shivering, with no one there
to calm her down
when she needed it most.

She must have whined
for a long time, while wires
taped to her skin
relayed her reactions.

She must have thought
it was some sort of game
gone painfully wrong
and that very soon they'd
release her.

She must have closed her eyes
when the temperature rose.
I hope she was thinking of trees,
of running through forests.

And if only they'd had the means
to bring her back,
she would have given them
her usual welcome,
forgiven them too,
like dogs forgive all humans,
the hurtful things they do.

TO THE MOON

It has been just the luck of a privileged few
to walk on the moon and look back at the view,
to stare at the planet they left behind
and to wonder if anything else they could find
would ever be quite so breathtaking as this,
no fast car ride, no daughter's kiss,
could ever come close to this mountain top,
this pinnacle, this unearthly drop.

And then after the tears and the interviews
and the general hullabaloo,
and the hundreds of times you walk through a door
to talk on TV and describe what you saw,
the realization still hits far too soon,
what do you do now you've been to the Moon?

DEAR YURI

Dear Yuri, I remember you,
the man with the funny name
who the Russians sent into space,
were you desperate for fame?

There surely must have been safer ways
to get into the history books,
perhaps you couldn't rock like Elvis
or you hadn't got James Dean's looks.

Perhaps you couldn't fight like Ali
or make a political speech
so they packed you into a spaceship
and sent you out of Earth's reach.

And Yuri, what was it like
to be way out there in space,
the first to break free of Earth's gravity
and look down on the human race?

Dear Yuri, I wanted to say
that I remember your flight,
I remember your name, Gagarin,
and the newsreel pictures that night.

And you must have pep talked others
when they took off into the blue.
I've forgotten their names, but Yuri,
I'll always remember you.

ALIENS STOLE MY UNDERPANTS

To understand the ways
of alien beings is hard,
and I've never worked it out
why they landed in my backyard.

And I've always wondered why
on their journey from the stars,
these aliens stole my underpants
and took them back to Mars.

They came on a Monday night
when the weekend wash had been done,
pegged out on the line
to be dried by the morning sun.

Mrs. Driver from next door
was a witness at the scene
when aliens snatched my underpants –
I'm glad that they were clean!

It seems they were quite choosy
as nothing else was taken.
Do aliens wear underpants
or were they just mistaken?

I think I have a theory
as to what they wanted them for,
they needed to block off a draught
blowing in through the spacecraft door.

Or maybe some Mars museum
wanted items brought back from Space.
Just think, my pair of Y-fronts
displayed in their own glass case.

And on the label beneath
would be written where they got 'em
and how such funny underwear
once covered an Earthling's bottom!

CLOSER TO HOME . . .

EMPTY PLACES

I like empty places.

The woods, the stream, the fields.

It's knowing I've no need
to make connections with anyone
about anything.

It's knowing I don't have to speak,
and that no one can contact me.

And the places themselves
are secure in their silence.
The landscape keeps tight-lipped,
it has no wish to reveal
its secrets.

(Although, just occasionally
I detect the whisperings of leaves,
the gossip of greenery.)

There are times, of course,
when my fingers feel the pulse of the city,
when its heartbeat connects with mine.
There are times too
when I need to be vocal,
when I need to crack the surface of silence.

But then it's back to those empty places,
that desire to be somewhere where no one else is,
to feel, to touch, to surf the breeze.

I like empty places,
the woods, the stream, the fields,
those kinds of places
that I can fill
with my dreams.

SOMETHING WRONG

Opening up the hen house
it's obvious something's wrong.

One chicken's in the nest box,
stiff to the touch.
Our first casualty
in eighteen months
just had to be Dora.

Night-time too,
cold January.
Closing them up for the night
I wasn't prepared.

Dora who gobbled sunflower seeds
till she squawked and hooted
like a blocked trumpet.

Dora who grew fat
on a diet of wriggly things,
who caused a riot in the garden
when she raced like a scrum half
with a slow worm.

And I always thought
how good it was to have
a long, long garden,
till I took that walk

back from the black
towards the light.

Holding my secret,
hugging it close.

At that moment,
no one else knowing
that Dora was dead.

ZOO OF WINDS

Wild winds have escaped tonight,
and like animals suddenly loose from a zoo
they are out doing damage.
We hear them snaking
into cracks and crevices
while beasts
with the strength of buffaloes
batter the building.
Shrill birds whistle through the hallway
and a lion's roar seems stuck
in the chimney.
A howling hyena is caught
in the porch
while a horrid hook of a claw
tries to splinter the loft hatch.
All manner of fearsome creatures
lunge down the lane
while our garden is buffeted
by the angry breath of bears.
I hope someone soon
recaptures these beasts,
locks them away,
cages them tightly.
These winds are not welcome visitors,
not tonight, not any time.

SEND A COW TO AFRICA

I found a cow in the field behind my house,
and as the farmer seemed to have lots of them
I thought surely he won't miss one.
So I took the cow to the Post Office.
'Send this cow to Africa,' I said.

The man behind the counter wasn't happy.
'You could have put a nappy on this cow
before you brought her here,' he said.

'And besides,' he continued. 'You can't
send a cow to Africa.'

'Why not?' I asked.

'Because it's noisy and it's messy
and it's likely to get stressy.'

'You just can't do it,
there'd be nothing for it to chew, it
would starve before it got there.
And besides, it would be smelly.'

'It'll be bored, and someone might
get gored. The horns are a problem,
you see. No matter which way it's wrapped
they'll still stick out.'

'But I need to send this cow,' I said,
'And I don't care how much it costs,
as long as I can fill in a form
for if it gets lost.'

'Listen,' the man said. 'There's no way
we can send this cow. Not now
or any other day.'

'That's OK,' I said. 'I understand.
I'll send a goat to India instead!'

A CAT CALLED ELVIS

(A cat called Elvis moved in next door . . .)

Elvis is Elvis before he joined the army.

No Vegas cat, fat and fortuned,
he's lean and mean,
a sneer on his face.

Kills birds,
knocks 'em dead.

A cat to be scared of,
a twist of the hip,
a curl of the lip.

No diplomat,
he's a rock 'n' roll cat,

A cat on the wall,
caterwauling.

Bad news for any dog
who steps on his
blue suede shoes!

WHITE HORSE

As a child I dreamed
a white horse would come
and carry me away.
Not that my childhood was unhappy,
it was just that my small-boy head
was full of adventures.
The horse was a noble beast,
perhaps a unicorn
in a previous existence,
an elemental creature
of ice and fire,
with a mane like a shower of stars.

I believed I had only to wish for the horse
and we'd flee over fields
to the sea, or rescue princesses
from castle towers
before galloping a path to the clouds.
And there were those moments
when the sky conjured up
a rainbow bridge,
where we may have passed
from this world to the next.

Later I discovered
that the white horse
wasn't rooted in childhood.
I came to realize

it had often been with me.
All those occasions
I'd wished to escape
and then found it.
All those times I'd flown
without knowing
I was riding the white horse's back.

Till now, with a different view
from a different house,
a white horse
paces the field beyond my window.
It seems to recognize in me
some previous complicity.
We were partners once,
we flew as one,
past the rim of what we knew
and out along the edges of dreams.

I DON'T WANT TO BELIEVE WHAT I'M TOLD . . .

NAMES

My name is 'Couldn't care less',
just let the forests die.
My name is 'Can't be bothered',
who cares about holes in the sky?

My name is 'I'm too busy',
let someone else do the worrying,
there's nothing that I can do
if the ice caps are wearing thin.

My name is 'Leave me alone',
just don't go preaching to me.
Gossip is what I care about
not oil that's spilt in the sea.

My name is 'I'm all right Jack',
there's really no cause for alarm.
Hens are silly birds, who cares
if they suffer at the factory farm?

Who cares about global warming,
I like a spot of hot weather.
My name is 'Sit on the fence',
my name is 'All of a dither'.

So stop saying what I should think,
I don't want to believe what I'm told.
My name is 'Hope it will go away',
My name is 'Don't get involved'.

And who do you think you are,
telling us all we should worry?
WELL MY NAME'S A WARNING FROM FUTURE
    YEARS,
IT'S 'LISTEN OR YOU'LL BE SORRY'.

THE LOST ANGELS
(France 1996)

In a fish tank in France
we discovered the lost angels,
fallen from heaven and floating now
on imaginary tides.
And all along the sides of the tank,
faces peered, leered at them,
laughing, pouting,
pointing, shouting,
while hung above their heads, a sign,
'Ne pas plonger les mains dans le bassin,'
Don't put your hands in the tank –
the turtles bite seriously.
And who can blame them,
these creatures with angels' wings,
drifting past like alien craft.
Who knows what signals they send
through an imitation ocean,
out of sight of sky,
out of touch with stars?

Dream on, lost angels,
then one day, one glorious day,
you'll flap your wings
and fly again.

CLASSROOM GLOBE

We strung our globe from the rafters
then watched as the continents spun.
We were dizzy with faraway places,
they swam before our eyes.
Everyone wanted to take a swipe at
the planet, to roll the world, to cause
global chaos. We laughed at the
notion of some great hand, sweeping down
avalanches, rolling earthquakes round
Africa, knocking elephants off their feet.
Then reasons were found for leaving seats,
to touch, or tilt, or hit heads on the planet,
squaring up to the world like March hares.
We talked of how the earth had been damaged,
leaving it bruised, sore from neglect,
and Jenny who feels sorry for anyone and
anything, leant her brow against the planet
and felt the sorrow and pain of Earth
in a cold hard globe.

MAKE FRIENDS WITH A TREE

Give a tree a squeeze,
give a tree a hug,
join in celebration
with every bird and bug,

with every bat and badger,
with beetles and with bees,
a new year's resolution,
show kindness to the trees.

> *Make friends with a tree,*
> *make friends with a tree,*
> *hug a tree, go on show it*
> *you really care, let a tree know it.*
> *Make friends with a tree,*
> *make friends with a tree.*

Trees are always homes
to every sort of creature.
In a flat and empty landscape
a tree is a special feature.

Trees can be deciduous,
pine trees are coniferous,
but trees will never hurt you
no tree is carnivorous!

So treat a tree politely,
show it you're sincere.
Long after we have disappeared,
trees will still be here.

> *Make friends with a tree,*
> *make friends with a tree,*
> *hug a tree, go on show it*
> *you really care, let a tree know it.*
> *Make friends with a tree,*
> *make friends with a tree.*

Snuggle up to a sycamore,
cuddle up to a pine
wrap your arms around an oak,
enjoy a joke with a lime.

A tree will always listen,
tell your troubles to a tree.
To the mystery of life
an ash may hold the key.

So don't be abrupt with a birch,
don't try to needle a pine.
Don't interrupt a horse chestnut,
don't give a tree a hard time.

Make friends with a tree,
make friends with a tree,
hug a tree, go on show it
you really care, let a tree know it.
Make friends with a tree,
make friends with a tree.

A tree is a living thing,
it's not just a lump of wood.
Trees in Sherwood Forest
know all about Robin Hood.

A tree can tell us stories,
a tree knows history,
so in this world of fake and sham
let's celebrate truth in a tree.

Make friends with a tree,
make friends with a tree,
hug a tree, go on show it
you really care, let a tree know it.
Make friends with a tree,
make friends with a tree.

LAST TIME

Leaving Earth for the last time,
we're locking all the doors.
We're leaving the planet to fend for itself
now it's bruised and broken and sore.

The silence here is unreal
now that everything's shut down.
No noise from traffic or factories,
quietness covers each town.

No time for tears or regrets,
we just didn't listen enough.
The message was stark and clear,
the solution far too tough.

We hoped the scientists were wrong,
that they couldn't predict our fate.
We put off paying attention
until it was far too late.

The last spaceships are leaving now,
there's nothing more to be done.
No one can survive any more
beneath this scalding sun.

It's a strange and awful feeling
to be leaving the land of my birth,
maybe someday someone will find
a way to recycle the Earth.

IN ALL THESE LIVES I'VE LIVED BEFORE . . .

IN ALL THESE LIVES . . .

I've been heroes and heroines,
I've been Queens, I've been Kings.

I've been a foot soldier in the army of Bonaparte.
I've been Romeo having lost his heart to Juliet.
I've been a bare knuckled boxer looking for a fight.
I've been the Conqueror on the night before Hastings.
I have travelled with Amundsen, with Columbus and
    Marco Polo.
I have sailed solo into the eye of a cosmic storm.
I have whispered words into Shakespeare's muddled
    mind.
I have circled the world on the Golden Hind with Francis
    Drake.
I have fought alongside my mother as Boadicea's
    daughter.
I have witnessed the slaughter of the elephants in the
    Roman Colosseum.
I have shaken hands with the ones who imprisoned me.
I have journeyed as a refugee when my home has been
    destroyed.
I have tested atomic bombs in the desert of Nevada.
I have offered advice to Harold Hardrada when he tried
    to take York.
I've been the general when the peace treaty was signed.
I've been the one who was blind and the one who saw.

Yes, I've been many things and I've been more,
in all these lives that I have lived before.

*(In this poem you'll notice that the rhyme on every
second line occurs in the middle of the line and not at the
end. This is called writing cross rhymes.)*

STONEHENGE

I remember Stonehenge
in the days where you could still
get close to the stones.
I remember being there, seeing their bulk
and feeling their solid substance.
It was the past brought close,
I could hear the tick of time,
the heartbeat of history.

If only the stones were transmitters,
they could broadcast their story,
answer the 'whys' of Stonehenge,
why Salisbury Plain gained
such a monument, why it was built,
was it temple or tomb?

If only we could summon solutions
from the sky, the clouds, the hills,
from those witnesses to the march
of these monoliths, to their positioning
and their raising.

And if only we knew who built this circle,
who mourned the winter sun
as the solstice darkened the day.
Did they ever imagine the puzzle
they were leaving behind?

And I wonder again at the thread
between present and past,
at all those who have stood
by these stones, hoping to hear
some sort of message
to the living from the dead,
so one of history's mysteries
might be solved at last.

ODE TO A ROMAN ROAD

Oh magnificent road, how straight thou art,
Not a bend, a curve, a hill or a tree
To distract either chariot or cart
From purposeful and needful journey,
Where soldiers would march without fuss or fear
And rest from foot-slogging on grassy banks.
Commanders could see for miles around
Foes who were drawing near
And legions were readied in solid ranks,
While orders were given to stand ironbound.*

Oh road, you'll be remembered through history,
The skills of your builders will be acclaimed.
Many will marvel at the mystery
Of how rough and rugged landscape was tamed
By those who laboured with shovel and pick
To connect each town like links in a chain.
A pattern was laid and so to this day
Our own roads often stick
Closely to those of the Roman terrain.
Let's recognize those who showed us the way.

*ironbound (unyielding)

BATTLEFIELD

*(There are different opinions these days as to
where the Battle of Hastings actually took place.
One opinion is that it was fought where a
road and a roundabout now stand.)*

This place could be
the battlefield.

This could be the place
where Harold's army,
tired and footsore,
stood their ground
as William's army
bore down on them.

And it isn't hard to imagine
the ranting and roaring,
the flutter of pennants,
the pounding of hooves,
the clashing of swords,
and the frightened steeds
trampling warriors.

And then when it seemed
the battle might be won,
William's army feigned retreat.
History records how a shower
of arrows fired in the air
left Harold dying, his troops
leaderless.

It was all so long ago,
so many memories in the mist,
so many summers, frozen winters.
Who really cares if it was fought
elsewhere?

Yet I hear it still,
down the ages, drawn like the wind
in the wires.

But who will hear it
in years to come,
buried beneath layers of earth,
silenced by the thunder of wheels?

LOVE LETTER FROM MARY TUDOR TO HER HUSBAND, PHILIP OF SPAIN

Dear Philip, my Phil
    it's making me ill
to think that
    you don't love me.
I love you my dear
    but you're making it clear
that this marriage
    was not meant to be.

I'm here all alone,
    if only you'd phone,
send a pigeon
    or simply just write.
Invite me, please do,
    Ibiza with you
would soon set
    our marriage alight.

Dear Philip, my love,
    my sweet turtle dove,
I know it's with you
    I relate.
I wish you'd return
    and help me to burn
all those plotting
    against the state.

Everybody I know
    says you should go,
but I need you
    to give me an heir.
Do you think that I'm neater
    than a sweet señorita
or do your eyes
    wander elsewhere?

Dear Philip, I'm willing
    to share double billing,
if our love could be
    reignited.
Then our reign as one
    will be equal to none,
King and Queen of
    two countries united.

So Philip, my Phil,
    come home, say you will,
without you it's really
    quite scary.
Forsake sunny Spain
    for the cold English rain
and the arms of
    your loving wife, Mary.

(Spot the anachronism – something in the wrong time.)

WHAT ARE WE FIGHTING FOR?

What are we fighting for?
        We have to do or die.
What are we fighting for?
        We can't turn a blind eye.
What are we fighting for?
        To sleep safely in bed.
What are we fighting for?
        To keep away fear and dread.
What are we fighting for?
        To keep our children free.
What are we fighting for?
        To choose our own destiny.
What are we fighting for?
        Because there's nowhere to hide.
What are we fighting for?
        Because so many have died.
What are we fighting for?
        To challenge oppression.
What are we fighting for?
        To combat aggression.
What are we fighting for?
        To win us the war.
What are we fighting for?
        So there won't be any more.

What are we fighting for?

                    So that we can make sure.

What are we fighting for?

                    It's a war to end war.

What are we fighting for?

                    So we'll never need to say

What are we fighting for?

                    Again.

CHRISTMAS TRUCE
(Christmas 1914)

'Hey Tommy, you like tobacco?'
'Hey Fritz, have my bottle of beer.'
'It's Christmas Day,
goodwill to all men, so,
what are we doing here?'

And maybe it would have stopped
then & there,
once Tommy and Fritz had realized
that both were ordinary men.
Not devils in khaki
with horns and a tail,
that both had families,
girlfriends, wives,
that both were a long long way
from anywhere, anyone
called home.

And all that sad, strange Christmas Day,
Tommy and Fritz shook hands with each other,
sang together the Christmas songs
that both discovered they knew.
They joked with each other
through gestures and signs,
in a language that needed
no words.

Then a football was found
and they played a match,
two nations in the midst
of war, the score unimportant.

And it finished with a rifle shot
that sent men back to their dug-outs.
Shouts of 'Merry Christmas Tommy,'
and 'Happy New Year to you Fritz.'
'Meet you again tomorrow,
show you photos of my girl.'

But it wouldn't do,
for the guns to stay silent
or to think of your enemy
as friend.

The rules of war are
clearly defined,
and someone must win
in the end.

PALS

Harry and Spud, Rawlings and I,
we were pals.
We lived in the same street,
attended the same school.

When war broke out
we joined up.
Seemed right somehow,
the four of us, together,
doing our bit
for King and Country.

It was hard at first,
but there were laughs too.
Harry and Spud, Rawlings and I
helped each other through.

We sang the songs,
not tunefully, but
enthusiastically.
I remember Spud
serenading Harry:
'If you were the only girl
in the world,' he warbled,
till Harry thumped him.

And laughter was the key
to keep our spirits up
when all we had
to look forward to
was mud and blood and bullets.

No idea why I survived
and they didn't.
One of the lucky ones me,
kept my head
below the parapet
and somehow the bullets
passed me by.

I've lived in the same street
all my life, and every year, the wife
and I, stand here on Remembrance Day
while I say a prayer for Harry and Spud
and Rawlings.

I run my fingers
over the names, etched in stone,
remember where their lives were lost,
and how we won the war,
but at what cost?

ANOTHER WAR

It wasn't just a war between the Germans and the Brits
it was a war between the 'vackies' and the village kids.

It was a war of words, a war of stones,
it was a war that threatened broken bones.

It was village kids with faces of granite
as if they belonged to some other planet.

'Go back home, we don't want you here,
go back where you came from, disappear.'

It wasn't just a war between the Germans and the Brits
it was a war between the 'vackies' and the village kids.

It was 'us and them', it was 'them and us',
it was mud fights causing family fuss.

Kids were rolling around in the dirt,
thumping each other and getting hurt.

Bloody noses and cauliflower ears,
the noise of jeering and lusty cheers.

It wasn't just a war between the Germans and the Brits
it was a war between the 'vackies' and the village kids.

It was big 'uns bullying and little 'uns crying,
it was twisted arms and fists that were flying.

It was, 'See you later for a fight after school'
and 'Chicken if you don't show, that's the rule.'

'You vackies will regret ever leaving your town
because we're the gang here and we'll knock you down.'

And it wasn't just a war between the Germans and the
     Brits
it was a war between the 'vackies' and the village kids,
it was a war between the 'vackies' and the village kids.

vackies (evacuees)

MOLLIE

(Parents in the Channel Islands had to choose between keeping their children with them or sending them away to the UK. Many children travelled with their teachers and faced a long sea crossing followed by an even longer train journey to the north of England.)

It was fine, all the time
she had Mollie,
as much as a rough sea and
a bucking boat could ever be really fine.
Leaving Guernsey, that feeling
of being lonely, but not alone,
with friends, but not family.
She'd always travelled with her parents before
and now, she'd left them behind.

So she clutched the doll, held her close,
tried to smile, tried to eat something,
to look on the bright side, as Mum would say,
put a brave face on it.

But somewhere between the ship and the train,
on the rainy streets of Weymouth,
in the hustle and bustle of a hurried chase
to reach the station on time,
Mollie must have fallen from her pocket.

It wasn't till the train hissed and set off
that she realized Mollie was missing.
Her teacher's hugs, her soft voice,
the sympathy of her friends,
nothing could console her, the tears
ran fast and freely.

And in the hours and hours it took
for the train to steam its way north,
the loss of the doll seemed
a link in a chain, now broken.
She and her family driven apart.
They, still in danger on Guernsey,
while she journeyed on to find
a new home with strangers.

IMPROBABLE OR IMPOSSIBLE?

SPIDER-SWALLOWING

This may be something you do not know,
indeed, it may be something you do not wish to know,
but you are, almost certainly,
a spider swallower.

You don't know it's happening,
but be assured, it does.

It's easy to swallow mozzies or midges or flies,
you open your mouth to shout out something to your
    mates
and then before you know it,
something takes a nosedive
down the black hole of your throat.

But spider swallowing happens at night.

Fast asleep, you're on your back, mouth open,
when a spider that's been happily exploring your ceiling
suddenly sees your face from above and lets down a line.

Seeing the open trapdoor of your mouth, it thinks,
'I'll just slip inside.'

And at that moment when you feel something tickle
    your teeth,
your mouth snaps shut.

Then there's only one place for the spider to hide
so it carries on down into your insides
never to be seen again.

When you wake next morning you don't remember a
    thing,
but the fact is, **everyone swallows at least eight
    spiders**
in one lifetime!

A FISH VENTRILOQUIST

I wanted to be the world's first fish ventriloquist,
so I searched and searched for the sort of fish
that might share the spotlight with me,
till somewhere near the Caspian Sea
I spoke with a cod who had found God
but all he wanted to do was pray with me.
In Yokohama I came across a shark
who had the sort of cut and thrust for showbiz life
but was more concerned with finding a wife.
I found a plaice with the most expressive face
but when I tried to put words into her mouth
she spat them out. I found an eel
whose personality was electric, but she was too much
of a shocker for me. I trembled every time I touched her.
I found a pike I liked immensely, but
he didn't like me, spat in my eyes each time
I tried to handle him. There was a ray who I could pass
the time of day with and a monkfish had possibilities
till I discovered he had taken a vow of silence.

Then right at the end of my search when I thought
I'd be returning to puppets and dolls,
I found a fish that was perfect, but although I swam
with him, ocean after ocean, offered him money, fortune
and fame, his name in lights, a season in Vegas,
he stubbornly refused to be swayed.

People would have paid thousands for the illusion of a talking fish. In a world where we celebrate the sham and the fake, fish ventriloquism could have been my big break.

YOU CANNOT TAKE A LOBSTER THROUGH SECURITY

Had no trouble with lobsters when travelling British Rail,
and no one said we couldn't take the ferry,
but the airport officials, all told me with one voice,
'You cannot take a lobster through security.'

They asked all kinds of questions, 'Is it pink or is it red?
Is it peaceful, is it vicious, is it live or is it dead?'
But no one was prepared to waive the rules and give
permission for us both to go ahead.

But they took my little brother who was bawling
    constantly,
and they took our great-aunt Mabel who was more than
    ninety-three,
and they took a Sumo wrestler who was wider than a
    tree,
but they wouldn't take my lobster through security.

I explained how my lobster was no mean mobster,
how it wasn't some disguised terrorist,
But they said that rules were rules and my lobster had to
    stay,
till they'd come across some suitable checklist.

They hadn't any plans for the kind of body scans
that would illuminate crustaceans
and besides it might be hiding some item that it
    shouldn't
or the subject of some special travel ban.

But they took my little brother who was bawling
    constantly,
and they took our great-aunt Mabel who was more than
    ninety-three,
and they took a Sumo wrestler who was wider than a
    tree,
but they wouldn't take my lobster through security,
no, they wouldn't take my lobster through security.

*(Someone did actually try to take a lobster through
security at Guernsey airport. A goldfish, a briefcase filled
with bricks, a chainsaw and a partially frozen turkey have
also been confiscated from passengers' luggage at other
airports.)*

SHOPPING TROLLEY

Scoot down the aisles
in my shopping trolley,
I could go for miles
in my shopping trolley.

Never say excuse me,
never say please,
ram it in the back
of someone's knees.

You really won't
believe your eyes,
My shopping trolley's
been customized.

It's got bull bars
radio controls,
engine in the back
and it purrs like a Rolls.

It's got a Volvo chassis,
a velvet seat,
and around the store
it can't be beat.

It does somersaults
and big back flips,
roly-polys
and wheely dips.

It does over seventy
miles per hour
flashing past
in a burst of power.

Scoot down the aisles
in my shopping trolley,
I could go for miles
in my shopping trolley.

Never say excuse me,
never say please,
ram it in the back
of someone's knees.

ALL THE THINGS YOU CAN SAY TO PLACES IN THE UK

Always say 'Ta' to Leamington Spa,
say 'Have a nice day' to Whitley Bay.
You can shout 'What's new?' or even 'Howdo'
to inhabitants of Looe or Crewe.
You can tell the whole story in Tobermory,
say 'Hi' to Rye and 'Right on' to Brighton,
or call out 'Let's go' to Plymouth Hoe.
Talk through your dreams in Milton Keynes,
say 'It's all for the best' in Haverfordwest.
Always say 'Yes' when you visit Skegness
but only say 'No' in Llandudno.
Don't tell a lie to the Island of Skye
or say 'It smells' in Tunbridge Wells.
Don't talk rude if you're down in Bude
or start to get gabby in Waltham Abbey.
Don't ever plead in Berwick on Tweed
or say 'You look ill' to Burgess Hill.
You could lose your voice and talk with your hands
when you take a trip to Camber Sands,
but whatever you say just won't impress
the inhabitants of Shoeburyness.

MONSTER CRAZY

Everyone here has gone Monster Crazy,
even those who are normally lazy,
binoculars raised, though the view may be hazy,
everyone here has gone Monster Crazy.

So come on Nessie, give us a wave,
don't stay hidden in your underwater cave.
You're the talk of the town, the darling of the press,
it wouldn't be summer without you in Loch Ness.

Just come on up and prove that you're there,
sometime or other you must surface for air,
somebody's camera will photograph you,
proving, at last, if you're one hump or two!

Everyone here has gone Monster Crazy,
even those who are normally lazy,
binoculars raised, though the view may be hazy,
everyone here has gone Monster Crazy.

Just waggle your flipper or flip your tail,
make some fisherman's face turn pale
as you lift your head to look at the view,
there are hundreds waiting to interview you.

Just one word Nessie, go on be a pet,
can't you stop playing hard to get?
You could be on TV, you'd have lots of money,
with American tourists calling you 'Honey!'

Everyone here has gone Monster Crazy,
even those who are normally lazy,
binoculars raised, though the view may be hazy,
everyone here has gone MONSTER CRAZY!

IF HOUSES WENT ON HOLIDAY

Wouldn't it be great
if when you went on holiday
your house could go on holiday too?
Whole terraces could disappear together
for boozy weekends in Ibiza.
Semi-detacheds could rekindle romance
side by side on moonlit beaches.
You'd find bungalows backpacking
and chalets criss-crossing the Channel.
Detached houses going solo,
seeking dates or mates on singles trips,
while apartment blocks could take package tours,
jetting to Jamaica in jumbos.

Just imagine houses hitting the holiday trail,
forming orderly queues on major roads
then crowding holiday beaches.
Imagine houses surfing or sunbathing,
jumping into swimming pools, keeping cool.
See them paragliding or rock climbing,
scuba diving or horse riding.
So much better than brooding, silent and empty,
rooms filled with gloom, windows
like sad eyes, blinking back tears.
How much better it would be for houses
to have holiday breaks like us.

HANG-GLIDING OVER ACTIVE VOLCANOES

It was truly amazing the first time I dared,
like surfin' in a furnace, but wow, was I scared!
That first time I tried it, I nearly died,
grilled to perfection on the underside.

Yes, I got singed from my eyebrows to my toes
from hang-gliding over active volcanoes.

I saw bubbling lava, fountains of fire,
felt warm blasts lifting me even higher.
I was floating along on waves of steam
while applying layers of suntan cream.

Yes, I got singed from my eyebrows to my toes
from hang-gliding over active volcanoes.

And it didn't take long to get me really hooked
on that great sensation of feeling half cooked.
What a thrill, I could chill in this situation
if I don't succumb to asphyxiation.

Yes, I got singed from my eyebrows to my toes,
I got scorched from my kneecaps to my nose
from hang-gliding over active volcanoes.

I NEVER
EXPECTED
FIREFLIES . . .

THE SONG
(Dublin 2002)

I came to Dublin to look for the song,
for some wayward melody
that, once heard, would be remembered,
but the song discovered me.

It was a message from a busker
in the hustle of Grafton Street,
I caught it escaping from doorways,
picked it up in the rhythm of feet.

I heard it splash in the Liffey,
I heard its blah! blah! blahs!
Every night it was telling wild stories
in a hundred smoky bars.

I heard it midnight drunk
till it sounded like a threat,
a bruised and broken version,
one that I'd rather forget.

I pursued it over a bridge
and up the Winding Stair,
then lost it in Quayside traffic
but couldn't abandon it there.

I caught it again in a saxophone
blowing such an aching tune,
I heard African drumbeats lift it up
and bounce it off the Moon.

It hid from me on O'Connell Street,
became part of the evening crowd,
then revealed itself in Temple Bar,
bold and brash and loud.

And it knows it can never be captured,
it demands its freedom to roam,
but I'm hoping still that a part of the song
will follow me back home.

MOON OVER MADRID

There's a moon over Madrid tonight,
a bright, inquisitive moon
that's about as full as it gets.
For me, it's something familiar
in an unfamiliar city,
a reference point on these Spanish streets.
It keeps me company, sometimes slipping
out of sight, dodging behind buildings
then reappearing, while I'm thinking
how the moon holds a thread
that ties us together.
'Look up at the moon,' I tell you.
'Look at the moon and imagine that thread
as a line linking you
to the mountains of the moon
and then down to the streets of Madrid.
That same moon touching your life,
now touches mine too.'

CONDOR
(Grand Canyon, Arizona)

You just can't whistle up a condor
from the Canyon,
they don't appear on demand.
That sort of magic
sneaks up on you,
surprises you
when your eyes are held
by Canyon colours,
the greens and the rust,
the bluest of skies.
When you're drawn to the drops
and the hide 'n' seek river,
It's then that something
will catch your eye,
the magic in black and white.
The flight of a bird
like some ancient Navaho apparition,
a feathered god, god of the sky,
now suddenly
brought back to life.

And then much later
when the holiday's past,
and the grey November days
signal summer has gone.
It's then that you'll stop
and remember
the touch of the Arizona sun,
and like a magician
you'll conjure up
the Canyon and the condor.

AMERICA'S GATE - ELLIS ISLAND

'I'm bringing something beautiful to America.'
(Girl, aged 10)

If I miss my name
    then I might be forever knocking
        on America's gate.
If I lose my ticket and miss my turn
    I may never learn the lie of this land.
For all I've planned
    is tied up in this trip,
all that I own
    is packed up in this bag.
And there isn't much money
    but there are gifts I can bring.
And I'm bringing them all to America.
I'm bringing them all from home.
Not my mother's rings
    or my party dress,
not my father's watch
    or my lacy shawl,
just the moon on my shoulder,
    a voice that can sing,
feet that can dance
    and a pipe that I play.
And I'm playing now for America,
    and I'm hoping that someone will notice.
Then perhaps I won't be here forever
knocking on America's gate.

FIREFLIES

(From the Observation Deck of the Empire State Building)

The guidebooks all said
the views were stupendous,
the moment momentous,
the light show tremendous,
but no one mentioned
the fireflies.

But the fireflies
are what I remember the most,
that aerial ballet of tiny sparks
that dipped and danced
and lit up the dark,
that hung a string of fairy-lights
in the sky above Manhattan.

And the light that flamed
from the streets below,
from the beating heart
of this electric city . . .
I wondered how many fireflies
it took, to stoke up that glow
and keep it burning.

I never expected fireflies
but then, New York's like that.

KIRK DEIGHTON

Kirk Deighton?
That can't be the name of a place.
Sounds more like the name
of a superhero, a '00' agent,
someone to swoon over.
Kirk Deighton,
suave, sophisticated,
a gold-plated gun in a
shoulder holster,
hairy chest, bulletproof vest.
The kind of guy that
girls adore, a secret spy on a
dangerous mission
somewhere off the A1,
South Yorkshire.

DUNGENESS

At first sight, the landscape
looks a mess,
like a giant's child dropping
his building bricks
and then kicking them around for a bit
to see where they settle.
People go there looking for
a different sort of somewhere,
it's that jumble sale kind of place
where you might just find anything.
The birds go more for order there,
neatly spaced seagulls on telephone wires,
pairs of pigeons on chimney pots.
Aside from a power station's paraphernalia
and two tubular light towers,
everything else crouches low,
grits its teeth, turns its back
on the winds that whip up the Channel.
A small train huff-puffs its way
along a single track;
It's either an ending or a beginning
depending on how you look at it.
It's a place without make-up,
no frills or fashions,
doesn't care if it's late,
can't be bothered to dress for dinner.
It's a take it or leave it
sort of place, no fuss.

But nevertheless, I like Dungeness.
I like the way it shrugs its shoulders,
couldn't care less.

THE BONFIRE AT BARTON POINT

The bonfire at Barton Point
was a wonderful sight, a spectacular blaze,
stuff legends are made of, wicked, ace!
We were talking about it for days.

There were beehives, signboards, slats and tables,
car tyres, a sledge and a wrecked go-cart,
a radiogram with a case of records,
some put-together furniture that must have pulled apart.

And like patients forsaken in mid operation
there were three piece suites in states of distress,
gashes in sides, stuffing pulled out,
and a huge Swiss roll of a mattress.

And we knew we'd need some giant of a guy
to lord it over a pile like this,
not a wimp in a baby's pushchair
that the flames would quickly dismiss.

But on the great and glorious night
we found it hard to believe our eyes
as tilted and tumbled on to the fire
came a whole procession of guys.

Then adults took over and just to ensure
the pile of guys would really burn,
they doused the heap with paraffin
so no ghost of a guy could return.

Then matches flared, torches were lit
at several points around the fire,
till suddenly everything caught at once
and fingers of flame reached higher.

And beaming guys still peered through smoke
till the fiery serpent wrapped them round
in coils of flame, and they toppled down
to merge with the blazing mound.

With our faces scorched, we turned away,
driven back by waves of heat
till after a time the fire slumped back,
its appetite replete.

Now as long as we live we'll remember
Barton Point with its fiery display
and the charred and blackened treasures
that we pulled from the ashes next day.

ONCE UPON A TIME THERE WERE UNICORNS . . .

LOST MAGIC

Today I found some lost magic –
a twisty-twirly horn
of a unicorn lying at my feet.
And when I stopped
to pick it up, to hold it
in my fist, I remembered
how once upon a time
you could always find unicorns,
but there are no unicorns now.

You would find them on the shoreline,
flitting in and out of caves in cliffs,
or climbing hills at twilight.
They would lead you through forests,
sometimes hiding behind trees,
and if you lost them or they lost you,
you could always find them again,
but there are no unicorns now.

And it didn't matter
if you followed them all day,
the edge of the world was miles away,
there was nothing to fear.
And none of the unicorns we knew ever
changed into dangerous strangers.
Once upon a time there *were* unicorns
but there are no unicorns now.

PLAYING WITH STARS

Young children know what it's like
to play with stars.

First of all it's a wink and a smile
from some distant constellation,
then it's hide-and-seek as they disappear
in a cover of cloud.
Sometimes children see how far
they can travel to a star
before familiar voices call them
home to bed.

Like all good games, of course,
you need to use a little imagination
when playing with stars.
More experienced players
can jump over stars
or shake down a star.
Some can trap them in butterfly nets,
but you should always let them loose again.
Stars grow pale and die if you cage them.

Sometimes the stars tell stories
of their journeys across the sky
and sometimes they stay silent.
At these times children may travel themselves,
wandering a line that unravels
through their dreams.
At these times too, the stars play their own games
falling from the sky when there's no one there
to catch them.

Sometimes you find these stars on the ground,
dazed, confused. Be warned though,
even fallen stars may be hot to touch.

Young children know what it's like
to rescue stars, to hold them gently
in gloved hands and then,
with one almighty fling,
sling them back to the sky.

Adults forget what it's like
to play with stars
and when children offer to teach them,
they're far too busy.

PARADISE STREET

Paradise Street in our town
was a street you didn't go down.

All the boys I was warned not to play with
lived on Paradise Street.

All the boys who swore,
who wore scars like fashion accessories,
who didn't need a reason to beat you up
or knock you down,
they all lived on Paradise Street.

Each season, a different torture.
In winter it was snowballs with sharp icy hearts,
In spring, they'd fling frogspawn.
Summer they dropped water bombs,
Autumn they were deadly with conkers.

Bogeymen, werewolves, vampires, the undead,
all the nightmares I dreaded
all started on Paradise Street.

Paradise Street was a shortcut
that nobody took,
where nobody went at night.

The lights were smashed
on Paradise Street,
it was doubly dangerous in the dark.

And when I think back
to Paradise Street,
I wonder who it was who gave it
such a crazy name.

Paradise Street
wasn't paradise
for anyone I knew.

NO ORDINARY STREET

I want to live in Polecat Alley,
I want to live in Dead Dog Lane,
don't want to live in an ordinary street
with some ordinary name.

I want to live in Mermaid Rise,
I want to swap my feet for a tail.
I want to hop all the way to Frog Street
and wait each day for my snail mail.

Don't want to live on East or West Street,
don't want to live on North or South.
I want a street that yells out loud,
a street that shoots off its mouth.

I want to live in Dragon Crescent,
see the night lit up by fire.
I want to live in Phoenix Close,
see new life rise from a funeral pyre.

What a pain it would be to live on School Lane,
a complete disaster, no fun at all.
But Dreamland Drive, that would be something,
surf and sunshine wall to wall.

Don't want to live on East or West Street,
don't want to live on North or South.
I want a street that yells out loud,
a street that shoots off its mouth.

I want to go mad in Crazy Lane,
lose my head in Boleyn Place.
On Harebeating Drive I don't think I could
give overgrown rabbits a punch in the face.

Dumpton Road would leave me depressed,
on Cross Street I'd grumble and grouse.
But Unicorn Avenue, that would be magic,
the perfect place to have my house.

Don't want to live on East or West Street,
don't want to live on North or South.
I want a street that yells out loud,
a street that shoots off its mouth.

I want to live in Polecat Alley,
I want to live in Dead Dog Lane,
don't want to live in an ordinary street
with some ordinary name.

(All the names of streets mentioned in this poem exist
and I actually lived on Harebeating Drive for seven
years!)

THE SKELETON IN
THE CUPBOARD

I heard my mother say
that the lady across the road
had a skeleton in her cupboard.

Immediately, of course,
I wanted to see it,
to rattle its bones,
to run my fingers
over its ribcage.

I wanted to snap its jaw,
to touch its teeth,
to make its feet
hit the floor
in a clitter-clatter
of bone on board.

But when I asked
the lady across the road
if I could see the skeleton
in her cupboard,
she wasn't pleased at all,
she shooed me away.

And when I told my mum
that I'd asked
the lady across the road
if I could see
the skeleton in her cupboard,
she wasn't pleased either.

I'm not allowed out now, Mum says.
So instead, I'm searching our cupboards
trying to find some whitened bones
of our own.

(*To have a 'skeleton in your cupboard' really means
to have a secret in your past that you probably
wouldn't want people to know about.*)

FIRE

There was a fire in our house
when I was a boy,
a living, breathing family fire
that we'd sit in front of,
warming feet or hands
in cold weather.
We'd be blocking the heat
from the rest of the room
till Dad would say, 'Let's feel
the warmth.' Or if we forgot
to close the door he'd yell,
'Were you born in a barn?'
or, 'Put the wood in the hole,
keep the heat in.'
It was true what he said,
heat would leave through
an open door, and even a closed room
would have cold spots,
icy places where you never
felt warm at all.
There were compensations of course
in stories by the fire, figures
in the flames, shadows dancing
on the walls, muffins
held against the embers
till they toasted.
Nothing like that these days.
Coming home, coming in from

the street, to be met
by the warmth from radiators
with a cosy and safe sort of heat
that could never fuel
the imagination.

ONLY A WARDROBE

In the end, it was, unfortunately,
only a wardrobe,
although hopes had been raised
that it could have been
an alternative route to Narnia.
For one thing, the wardrobe was old,
ancient in fact, woodwormed
and waiting, surely, for four children
to come adventuring.
It was spacious too, and there were coats
and empty hangers that clanged
as they pushed past them.
But for Sharon and Tracey, Gavin and
Isaac, it was disappointing.
They'd hoped for snow, a few flakes
at least to show they were on the right track
but they'd not even felt cold.
They'd tapped and pushed and stamped,
hoping to discover a secret spring,
a trapdoor, an entranceway,
but nothing happened, no exciting window
to another world.
The wardrobe was simply a hollow space
and they'd just have to face it, life was dull,
adventures only happened on the screen,
in books, to others; they weren't for them.
In the end it was only a wardrobe
and I'd be lying to you if I said they found Narnia,

or indeed if any of us have.
The best secrets stay hidden, hidden deep,
but there is, and must always be,
something to search for,
always that slim chance.

GRAFFITI BOY

I'm Rory, yeah, and since I was a boy
I've been writing my name everywhere I go,
it was Rory in the wet sand,
Rory in the snow.
Rory scuffed in gravel,
Rory scrawled on walls.
I chalked my name on pavements,
in schools and shopping malls.
I've been marking out my territory
and others had better beware:
these streets belong to Rory,
challenge me if you dare.

Rory tells my story,
it speaks my history.
Read my name and wonder
at this man of mystery.

Now my story's moved up a notch
as I spray my name these days.
I'm the aerosol king of the junction
with my artistic displays.
And I love to travel about
noticing my name,
it gives me a heck of a buzz,
it gives me a taste of fame.
It's great when I'm walking a street,
knowing that round the next bend

is a place where I wrote my name,
it's like meeting up with a friend.

Rory tells my story,
it speaks my history.
Read my name and wonder
at this man of mystery.

I'd like to see my name in lights,
I'd like to see it glow
and sometimes at night I imagine
the stars put on a show.
And looking up at the sky
you can guess at my elation,
my name across the heavens
in a brand-new constellation.
It's the ultimate piece of graffiti
that no one else could top.
I'd be Rory, universally,
end of story, full stop.

BILLY'S COMING BACK

Word is out on the street,
Billy's coming back.

There's a sound outside of running feet,
somebody, somewhere's switched on the heat,
policemen are beating a swift retreat
now Billy's coming back.

Only last year when he went away
everyone heaved a sigh,
now news is out, and the neighbourhood
is set to blow sky-high.

Words are heard in the staffroom,
teachers' faces deepen with gloom,
can't shrug off this feeling of doom,
now Billy's coming back.

It was wonderful when he upped and left,
a carnival feeling straightaway,
no looking over shoulders,
each day was a holiday.

And now like a bomb, no one dares to defuse,
time ticks on while kids quake in their shoes
no winners here, you can only lose,
now Billy's coming back.

It's dog eat dog on the street tonight,
it's cat and mouse, Billy's looking for a fight,
so take my advice, keep well out of sight
now Billy's coming back.

THE HATE

We began each morning with hymns,
'Lots of wind,' our teacher called
as she wrestled a melody
from the ancient hall piano.

Then we sat and gazed at the front
while the football results were read
and Donald was led in, held by the arm,
a look of alarm on his face.
I didn't know what he'd done,
perhaps he'd stolen or two-fingered
once too often. It must have been serious
in the eyes of God, in the eyes
of our headmistress.

She seemed to think
that boys' backsides were meant to be whacked,
but Donald struggled and lay on the floor
and flapped like a fish out of water.
Even the toughies were terrified
as the slipper rose and fell
a total of eighteen times till it stopped
and Donald stayed locked to the floor.

The piano was open but no one played
as we filed out silently and found our maths.
It stayed on our minds for much of the day
but Donald wouldn't say what he'd done
just shook his head and said nothing.

Our teacher said Donald would be forgiven,
start once again and clean the slate;
but I glimpsed him next day in prayers,
a dreadful look on his face, and I knew
it would take more than Jesus
to wipe away the hate.

HOLDING THE HANDS OF ANGELS

It's the sort of thing
I look back on now and think, 'Wow,
what was I doing?'
Climbing some cliff face,
risking my life
and for what?

It was dares, of course,
dares and challenges.
Chicken if you didn't,
so we did.
Bet you can't climb to that ledge,
bet you can't reach that cave.

And it was miraculous
that nothing happened.

It wasn't till now
that I realized why.
We must have been
holding the hands
of angels.

All those times
we wriggled back,
a hair breadth from disaster,
cut and scratched,
sticky-plastered.

Angels were watching us,
guiding our feet,
pulling us back
from the lightning crack of ice
on a frozen lake.

We believed ourselves invincible,
didn't think how
water drowns,
bones break,
skulls crack . . .

It's the sort of thing
I look back on now and think, 'Wow,
what was I doing?'

A TIME ERASER

Wouldn't it be great
to be able to roll back time
and revisit what we were,
to make amends for what we did wrong,
to refashion what we've become,
get rid of those cringe-making moments
with one stroke of an eraser?

Wouldn't it be great if life was just a first draft?
Like a piece of writing that you could go back
and tidy up before you presented it.
Hurtful words could be removed,
more sensitive sentences inserted.

I'd love to be able to cut and paste my life,
to lose the daft bits, the sad bits,
the excruciatingly awful bits.
That girl I asked for a date and she said no.
In the revised life that I devised
she'd immediately agree.
And that ball I kicked through the window
could be booted back, with the window unbroken,
not even a crack.

That easy question I fluffed in the maths lesson,
letting the teacher know that I knew absolutely
nothing at all. No worries now,
a quick flick will rub it out and get rid
of my red face.

Wouldn't it be great to do all that,
to just wind back and change the days,
to give myself a good-as-new life,
one that wouldn't embarrass me?

(Anyone lend me that sort of eraser,
I'd really be very grateful?)

HOW COOL IS SCHOOL?

TARGETS

My teacher says my targets are:

To write more neatly,
to spell more words correctly,
to get more sums right,
to chatter less,
and to behave myself.

But the targets I set myself
are far more interesting:

To climb a tree to the top,
to stop time before my spelling test,
to think up a disappearing spell
and try it out on my teacher,
to leap from up high
and to defy gravity.

These are my targets,
the ones I'm aiming to complete
before next week . . .

The ones my teacher sets
may take a little longer . . .

WHAT TEACHERS WEAR IN BED

*(After overhearing a conversation between six teachers
in the staffroom at . . . school. Sssh! Better not say
which one, it could be yours . . . !)*

It's anybody's guess
what teachers wear in bed at night,
so we held a competition
to see if any of us were right.

We did a spot of research,
although some of them wouldn't say,
but it's probably something funny
as they look pretty strange by day.

Our head teacher's quite old-fashioned,
he wears a Victorian nightshirt,
our sports teacher wears her tracksuit
and sometimes her netball skirt.

That new teacher in the infants
wears bedsocks with see-through pyjamas,
our deputy head wears a T-shirt
he brought back from the Bahamas.

We asked our secretary what she wore
but she shooed us out of her room,
and our teacher said, her favourite nightie
and a splash of expensive perfume.

And Madamoiselle, who teaches French,
is really very rude,
she whispered, 'Alors! Don't tell a soul,
but I sleep in the . . . back bedroom!'

BEHIND THE STAFFROOM DOOR

Ten tired teachers slumped in the staffroom at playtime,
one collapsed when the coffee ran out, then there were
nine.

Nine tired teachers making lists of things they hate,
one remembered playground duty, then there were
eight.

Eight tired teachers thinking of holidays in Devon,
one slipped off to pack his case, then there were seven.

Seven tired teachers, weary of children's tricks,
one hid in the stock cupboard, then there were six.

Six tired teachers, under the weather, barely alive,
one gave an enormous sneeze, then there were five.

Five tired teachers, gazing at the open door,
one made a quick getaway, then there were four.

Four tired teachers, faces lined with misery,
one locked herself in the Ladies, then there were three.

Three tired teachers, wondering what to do,
one started screaming when the bell rang, then there
were two.

Two tired teachers, thinking life really ought to be fun,
one was summoned to see the Head, then there was one.

One tired teacher caught napping in the afternoon sun,
fled quickly from the staffroom, then there were none.

SHEEP WARS: THE DRAMA TEACHER'S DILEMMA!

'We need more lines for Sheep 2 to say,
he doesn't say enough in our Nativity play.
His parents will complain if Sheep 2 is too dumb,
if they think his importance is less than Sheep 1.
They're the sort of parents who will time how long
Sheep 2 is on stage compared with Sheep 1,
and whether he's centre stage or sidelined,
then demand his position be redefined.

So someone, please write more lines, and fast,
if Sheep 2's appearance on stage is to last
as long as Sheep 1 and then that will avoid
any trouble from his parents if they are annoyed.
The last thing we want is Sheep Wars to break out,
for the Sheepy parents to scream and shout.
This is, after all, the season of goodwill
so fill Sheep 2's mouth, let him speak until
the curtain comes down on our school play
and his parents, happy, lead him away.'

DAY CLOSURE

We had a day closure on Monday
and I spent the morning in bed,
but the teachers went in as usual
and someone taught them instead.

And I thought of them all in the classroom,
stuck to their seats in rows,
some of them sucking pen lids,
head teacher scratching his nose.

Perhaps it's a bit like an MOT
to check if teachers still know
the dates of our kings and queens
or the capital of so-and-so.

Perhaps they had tables and spellings,
did the Head give them marks out of ten?
And then, if they got any wrong,
did he make them learn them again?

I thought of them out at break-time
playing football or kiss chase or tag,
picking up teams in the playground
or scoffing crisps from a bag.

If I'd been a fly on the wall,
I might have watched while they slaved,
I'd have seen who asked silly questions
or if anyone misbehaved.

I thought of them all going home,
crossing the road to their mums.
They looked very grim the next day.
It couldn't have been much fun.

THE SCHOOL GOALIE'S REASONS . . . WHY EACH GOAL SHOULDN'T HAVE BEEN A GOAL IN THE MATCH THAT ENDED 14:0 TO THE VISITING TEAM

1. It wasn't fair. I wasn't ready . . .
2. Their striker was offside. It was obvious . . .
3. Phil got in my way, he always gets in my way, he should be dropped . . .
4. I had something in my eye . . .
5. I hadn't recovered from the last one that went in, or the one before that . . .
6. I thought I heard our head teacher calling my name . . .
7. Somebody exploded a blown-up crisp bag behind me . . .
8. There was a beetle on the pitch, I didn't want to tread on it . . .
9. Somebody exploded another blown-up crisp bag behind me . . .
10. That girl in Year Five was smiling at me. I don't like her doing that . . .
11. The goalposts must have been shifted, they weren't as wide as that before . . .
12. I thought I saw a UFO fly over the school . . .
13. There was a dead ringer for Jamie Vardy watching us, he was spooky . . .

And goal number 14?
It just wasn't a goal, I'm sorry, it just wasn't a goal
and that's that . . .
OK?

CAKES IN THE STAFFROOM

Nothing gets teachers more excited
than cakes in the staffroom at break-time.
Nothing gets them more delighted
than the sight of plates
piled high with jammy doughnuts
or chocolate cake.

It's an absolute stampede
as the word gets round quickly,

And it's 'Oooh these are really delicious,'
and, 'Aaah these doughnuts are great.'

And you hear them say, 'I really shouldn't'
or 'Just a tiny bit, I'm on a diet.'

Really, it's the only time they're quiet
when they're cramming cakes into their mouths,
when they're wearing a creamy moustache,
or the jam squirts out like blood,
or they're licking chocolate
from their fingers.

You can tell when they've been scoffing,
they get lazy in literacy,
sleepy in silent reading,
nonsensical in numeracy,
and look guilty in assembly.

But nothing gets teachers more excited
than cakes in the staffroom at break-time,
unless of course,
it's wine in the staffroom at lunchtime!

THE DEAD DON'T TELL TALES, OR DO THEY?

THE TRACKS AND THE TOMBSTONES

Our classroom lay between
the tracks and the tombstones.

On one side
electric trains
ploughed the line to London.
On the other
a graveyard
beckoned uninvitingly.

One offered hope,
climb on board, get away.
The other mocked,
don't bother, don't try.
This is your ultimate destination,
graveyard, not railway station.

One side was noisy.
Messages hummed in the rails:
A clatter on the tracks,
a zing in the lines,
a hell of an interruption.

The other was quiet,
not quiet quiet,
just lifeless.

And we could be lifeless too.
Our teacher would joke:
'There's more life out there
in that boneyard,
than there is in you lot today!'

But when we wanted,
we could be dead quick:
We'd play about
when the teacher was out,
knowing that no one
was keeping an eye . . .

Trains move too fast,
the dead don't tell tales.

Our classroom lay between
the tracks and the tombstones.
Our classroom lay between
the quick and the dead.

CAN GHOSTS KISS?

If one ghost fancied another
what would they do?

You wouldn't get all that kissy-wissy,
lip-smacking, thwacking, sucking sounds
with ghosts, would you?

It would be more like watching
a silent film, although there might be
a hiss when their lips met.

And would they feel anything at all?
Would one ghost know when he'd kissed
another? Could ghosts recall
the sensation they'd felt
when they were alive?

And what if you were a ghost without a head,
if you carried your head under your arm
and you fancied another ghost
with a head in a similar place?

Could two bodiless heads
still kiss?

Maybe the ghosts who were holding
their heads would tilt them sideways
like the living do.

And would they feel thrills
or just chills?

Would their lips be kissable,
the experience unmissable,

if one ghost fancied another?

THE HANGED MAN

I remember how Ben and I,
each summer morning, on our way to school,
would slip into the cool of
Gibbet's Wood, to find the hanged man's tree.
Nothing was certain but it seemed to us
the likeliest place, and it felt so too,
always chilly, always dark and far enough from the road
to be silent.

We'd stand and listen, imagining we heard
a rough word or two from centuries back,
thinking we could see bleached bones or
a skull picked clean by crows.
All I know is that it stayed in my head at night
and helped give shape to the shadows
in my room. Ben said he couldn't sleep,
his dreams were filled with dread.

We'd try to forget, leave it alone, run to school,
but it drew us back like an itch that
we couldn't stop scratching.
I could tell it was some sort of spell
that was holding us there, maybe a message
we needed to hear, but nothing appeared,
nothing summoned us.

Years later I stood by the tree once more,
felt the same pull, as if there were a doorway
I ought to pass through, knowing if I did,
I'd never return. I felt the hanged man's eyes
burning into my back as I fled. And I wish I'd known
    then,
what I realize now, no good could ever come
from spying on the dead.

HAUNTED HOUSE

Who it was, we never knew.
I heard footsteps, we all did too.
In the upstairs room, in the fading light,
something more at home with the night
crossed over that line between life and death,
making us tremble, holding our breath.
It happened the once, we never heard it again,
but once was enough, I was only ten
when I understood that nothing was certain,
a touch, a feeling, the flick of a curtain.

I looked over my shoulder for years, I still do;
there's a ghost of a chance that it might call on you.

DUNOTTER CASTLE

(Just south of Aberdeen)

This fortress that's built on a rock
is the spookiest of places,
where the Scots could retreat when attacked
and laugh in their enemies' faces.
It's empty now and quite forlorn
but it's still <u>the</u> castle to see,
roofless buildings, empty rooms
and a whiff of tragedy.

The rushing of winds in the ruins
have hollowed out its heart,
I imagine the rumble on flagstones
of a timeslipped horse and cart.
The pigeons in the tower
are spooked by my being here,
they take off and halo the castle
then swiftly disappear.

In the visitors' book someone wrote:
'It's a miracle, it really is brill,
it sent a chill through my blood,
today has been such a thrill.'
Someone else wrote, 'It's fabulous,
this castle is really the most,
taught us a lot about history,
but pity we missed the ghost!'

And as I left, with the day turned grey,
and the great door locked for the night,
I imagined not one ghost but hundreds
looking down from the castle heights.
An army of phantom warriors
ready once more to defend
their country from hostile invaders
in a fight to the bitter end.

ADVERTISEMENT FROM THE GHOSTLY GAZETTE

There's a special place where you can stay
when your haunting is over each night,
it's a spooky spooktacular guest house
where you'll sleep away the light.

In each room the curtains are shut
so the sun's rays never slip through.
We guarantee you a good day's sleep
with nothing disturbing you.

There's a hook on the back of your door
where if you've lost your head
your eyes can still watch over you
while your body rests in bed.

We have rooms with very tall ceilings
for ghosts who levitate
and to make you feel among friends
we can colour co-ordinate.

Grey ladies stay in one room
and green ladies in another.
Poltergeists are soundproofed
so they only disturb each other.

For those who like walking through walls
and would rather not use the door
Please feel free to enter this way
or even rise up through the floor.

We can cater for every need
and we're sure that you'll love it here.
Just don't forget to pay the bill
before you disappear!

GHOSTS OF THE LONDON UNDERGROUND

In the subway tunnels
dying to be found,
on the Circle Line
going round and round,
in the wail of the wind,
a peculiar sound,
these ghosts
of the London Underground.

Down, deep down, down deep underground
these ghosts of the London Underground.

And maybe you'll find
you can see right through
the passenger sitting
opposite you
or a skull appears
from beneath a hood
and you really wish
you were made of wood,
that you didn't see
what you think you did
and all these horrors
were still well hid.

Down, deep down, down deep underground
with ghosts of the London Underground.

No ticket needed,
you travel free
in the freakiest, scariest
company.
Stand clear of the doors
we're about to depart,
so block up your ears
and hope that your heart
is strong enough
to survive the ride,
we're taking a trip
to the other side.

*Down, deep down, down deep underground
with ghosts of the London Underground.*

And the tunnels echo
with demonic screams
that chill your blood
and drill into your dreams.
And you can imagine
only too well,
how these tunnels might lead you
STRAIGHT INTO HELL . . .

*Down, deep down, down deep underground
Down, deep down, down deep underground
Down, deep down, down deep underground
these ghosts of the London Underground.*

these ghosts . . .

these ghosts . . .

these ghosts . . .

THE PHANTOM KISS

There's a phantom kiss on the loose,
you could find it in your house.
It flits about like a fly,
it scuttles about like a mouse.
It hides in gloomy corners
till someone turns out the light,
so you won't be able to see it
in the darkness of the night.
But the phantom kiss will be there
and you won't hear it speak your name,
but if it calls and it touches you,
you will never be the same!

Like a vampire that turns you into its own,
the phantom kiss will claim you.
Just a gentle brush of lips on your cheek
is all that it takes to inflame you.
You'll be wanting to kiss
everyone you see,
be it greatest friend
or deepest enemy.

If the phantom kiss
holds you in its power,
you won't shrug it off
in a minute or an hour.
It will hold you tight
in its embarrassing grip
while you kiss all around you
on cheek or on lips.

So remember if your mum's
always kissing you,
you'll realize now
that she was touched too.
And serial kissers
like your aunts and your gran
you'll realize this
was how they began.

And someone who may have been touched too
is the person sitting next to you . . .

THE FEAR

I am the footsteps that crackle on gravel
and the sudden chill that's hard to explain.
I am the figure seen flitting through doorways
and the noisy rattle of a loose windowpane.

I am the scream that wakes you at night
with the thought, Was it real or a dream?
I am the quickening thud of your heart
and the feeling things aren't what they seem.

I am the slam of a door blown shut
when there isn't even a breeze
and the total and absolute certainty
that you just heard someone sneeze.

I am the midnight visitor,
the knock when there's no one there.
I am the ceiling creaking
and the soft footfall on your stair.

I am the shadows that dance on your wall
and the phantoms that float through your head.
And I am the fear that you feel each night
as you wriggle down deep in your bed.

THE PHANTOM FIDDLER

*(A ghostly apparition said to haunt
Threshfield School in the Dales)*

There can't be an apparition
in our school.
We have rules to stop anyone
getting in.
We have keypads and an intercom
to keep children from harm.
Yet it seems that something
has invaded our building,
something that I heard last night
as I scooted down the street.
A screeching sound
like a fiddler playing,
laying down a curious tune
by the light of a magical moon.

And as I peered through the window,
into the gloom of 3B's room,
I caught a glimpse of children,
or were they imps,
dancing round to the sounds
a fiddler played.
And I had to admit
that the music captured me.
And I danced to the fiddler's tune
by the light of a magical moon.

Sensible people would have scuttled by,
they wouldn't have lingered like I did.
They wouldn't have looked in the fiddler's eye
or followed when he crooked his finger.
And I had no choice but to stay with him
as I danced to the tune he played
and the imps came too
as we danced in the street
by the light of a magical moon.

But something must have broken the spell,
something must have woken me up.
And I saw the imps for what they were,
nasty, ghastly, horrid things
that chased me all the way to the well
where I leapt in the Holy Water.

* * * * * *

And that's where I was found
later that night,
when lights blazed over the hill,
shivering down in Lady's Well,
still hearing that phantom fiddler's tune
by the light of a magical moon.

THE WEIRDEST EXHIBIT

The museum galleries
go on for miles,
you see furniture and furnishings,
tapestries and tiles.
You see kitchens where fire grates
are blackened with soot,
but the weirdest exhibit
is a mummified foot.

It's gruesome and gross
but you'll love it the most,
the Egyptian mummified foot.

You can see right inside
where the skin has been ripped,
then you'll notice the bone
and the way it's been chipped.
And beneath the bandage
you'll see actual flesh . . .
I bet it smelt cheesy
even when it was fresh!

It's gruesome and gross
but you'll love it the most,
the Egyptian mummified foot.

And what's so amazing,
what's really fantastic,
the toenails are real
and not made of plastic.
And beneath the nails
you can see grains of sand.
Are they picked at each night
by a mummified hand?

It's gruesome and gross
but you'll love it the most,
the Egyptian mummified foot.

THE MUSEUM OF MYTHICAL BEASTS

Go right in, past a beam of light
that shoots from a Cyclops' eye,
then put on armour and pick up a sword,
test how much of a hero you are:
Only the bravest and best may steal the gold
from a griffin's nest.

Then try to resist a mermaid's song.
How long will you stay before you can bear
to block your ears and turn away.

Now braver souls have tangled with trolls,
they'll carry you off to be their slave.
Careful, don't trip, just a pile of old bones,
previous visitors, I suppose!

A date with Medusa! What a surprise!
Keep your head and don't look in her eyes.
Move forward once more till you reach a door.
The Minotaur is next on our list,
a horrible task, you'd be well advised
to go prepared when you visit his lair.

That terrible smell is the Gorgon of death;
run past, run fast, don't waste any time
in escaping the blast of its breath.

Beware the Roc that will carry you off
as a titbit for one of her young
or the goblins already crouched over their pans
or the two-headed ogre who can't decide
which mouth he should slide you in!

And now you come to the final test,
a dragon, so deadly, so dreadful, so strong.
Don't weaken at all when you hear her ROAR
as you score points with Saint George.

Then at the exit, don't forget
to collect your certificate,
dated and signed to say you survived
the museum of mythical beasts.

THE GHOUL-SCHOOL BUS

The ghoul-school bus
is picking up its cargo
of little horrors.

They must all be home
before first light, when today
turns into tomorrow.

All the sons and daughters of vampires,
little Igors and junior Fangs,
the teenage ghouls with their ghoulfriends
all wail as the bus bell clangs.

And the driver doesn't look well,
he's robed completely in black,
and the signboard says – Transylvania,
by way of hell and back.

The seats are slimy and wet,
there's a terrible graveyard smell,
all the small ghouls cackle and spit,
and practise their ghoulish spells.

The witches are reading their ABCs,
cackling over 'D' for disease,
while tomboy zombies are falling apart
and werewolves are checking for fleas.

When the bus slows down to drop them off
at Coffin Corner or Cemetery Gates,
their mummies are waiting to greet them
with eyes full of anguish and hate.

The ghoul-school bus
is dropping off its cargo
of little horrors.

They must all be home
before first light, when today
turns into tomorrow.

PARENTS, WHO NEEDS THEM?

LOVEY-DOVEY

When Dad and Mum go all lovey-dovey
we just don't know where to look.
My sister says, 'Cut it out you two,'
while I stick my nose in a book.

Mum has this faraway look on her face
while Dad has a silly grin.
'Don't mind us kids,' he says,
we just wish they'd pack it in.

Dad calls Mum, 'Little Sugarplum'
and Mum says, 'You handsome brute.'
Dad laughs and says, 'Look at your mum,
don't you think that she's cute?'

'I guess that's why I married her,
she's my truly wonderful one.'
Mum says he doesn't mean any of it
but she thinks he's a lot of fun.

I just can't stand all the kissing,
just who do they think they are?
I caught them once on our driveway
snogging in the back of our car!

I hate it when they're lovey-dovey
but I hate it more when they fight,
when faces redden and tempers flare
and sharp words cut through the night.

So I'd rather they kissed and cuddled
and joked about and laughed,
at least we can tell everything's OK
when Mum and Dad are daft.

A DAD REMOTE CONTROL

Our mum's got a dad remote control
that she points in his direction
whenever he slumps down on the settee
or starts to raise an objection.

She presses one button for 'walk the dog',
another for 'cook the tea'
and when she feels a little low
there's one labelled 'pamper me'.

Then there's 'run my bath' and 'pour my drink'
and 'time to stop lounging about'.
She presses a button for 'go and wash up'
and then 'take the rubbish out'.

And when she feels he should pay her attention
she operates 'please adore me'.
But when he goes on about football scores
she switches him off with 'you bore me'.

But when our mum goes out with her friends
and at last it's Dad's turn to choose,
he points the remote control at himself
and presses the button marked 'snooze'.

THE SHOUTING SIDE

There's a war being waged
in our family,
Mum versus Dad,
in the middle there's me
and it's hard to decide
whose side I'm on
when they're both
on the shouting side.

Dad shouts at Mum,
Mum screams at Dad,
then they start on me
and it makes me mad,
I don't want to decide
whose side I'm on
when they're both
on the shouting side.

Can't they see,
can't they be quiet?
Why do they yell
like they're starting a riot?
They're acting this out
on a tiny stage,
there's no need to shout
or fly into a rage.

There's no need to take out
their feelings on me,
I'm trying to listen,
can't they see.
I'm standing here
with my eyes wide open,
somebody please
be quietly spoken.

There's a war being waged
in our family,
Mum versus Dad,
in the middle there's me
and it's hard to decide
whose side I'm on
when they're both
on the shouting side.

PARENT-FREE ZONE

Parents please note
that from now on,
our room is
a 'Parent-Free Zone'.

There will be no spying
under the pretence
of tidying up.

There will be no banning
of television programmes
because our room
is a tip,

no complaints about noise,
or remarks about the ceiling
caving in.

No disturbing the dirty clothes
that have festered in piles
for weeks.

No removal of coffee cups
where green mould
has taken a hold.
(These have been left there
for scientific research purposes.)

No reading of letters
to gain unauthorized information
which may be used against us
at a later date.

No searching through school bags
to discover if we've done our homework
or unearth forgotten notes.

Our room is a 'Parent-Free Zone'
and a notice is pinned to the door.

But just a minute,
there's something wrong . . .

MUM – WHY HAVEN'T YOU MADE OUR BEDS?

EYES, WINGS, DRAGON FLAME . . .

DRAGONS' WOOD

We didn't see dragons
in Dragons' Wood
but we saw
where the dragons had been.

We saw tracks in soft mud
that could only have been left
by some sharp-clawed creature.

We saw scorched earth
where fiery dragon breath
had whitened everything to ash.

We saw trees burnt to charcoal.
We saw dragon dung
rolled into boulders.

And draped from a branch
we saw sloughed off skin,
scaly, still warm . . .

We didn't see dragons
in Dragons' Wood,
but this was the closest
we'd ever been

to believing.

THE DRAGONS ARE HIDING
(Written near Machynlleth, Mid-Wales)

To be born a dragon hunter
is somehow to know, that once,
a very long time ago, dragons
were not just the stuff of dreams.
It was a way for young men
to fulfill their destinies, to ride off
on horseback, seeking treasure.
It was, first and foremost,
a measure of their courage,
the best sort of quest.

It was a solitary pursuit, one to one,
hunter and hunted, the odds even.
Sharp eyes, cunning and surprise
all counted, for a lick of flame
would be all it took to paralyse.
Dragons knew they were young men's
quarry, they became elusive, led
secluded lives, slept by day, fed
at night, easily fled when challenged.

Then down the years, dragons
disappeared. There were tales
of course, a mountain in Scotland,
a labyrinth in Wales, but the trails
proved cold; no smoke-blackened
caves, no burnt-out villages,
no graves of would-be dragon
hunters.

Yet recently there were rumours again:
The whisper of wing-beats in darkness,
distant thunder from mountains,
a tumult beneath a waterfall where roaring
could easily be disguised.

Any young warrior out seeking dragons
should look again, in slate caverns
and abandoned mine shafts.
They should travel to the hidden sides
of mountains, look beneath Devils'
bridges and dig down to discover
the silent secret spaces
where dragons might be waking.

For in a darkening Welsh landscape
with evening purpling the hills,
it is easy, so easy to believe
how those of us who would be
dragon hunters, could one day
find them again.

DRAGON PATH

(For Crowhurst village school, who gave this name to a path in their playground)

Nothing will be the same as before
once you've drawn a dragon to your door,
once a dragon knows just where to find you
you'll always have to look behind you,
always have to take great care
once you summon a dragon from its lair.
And it won't be any kind of joke
if you see flames, if you smell smoke
or wake to find in dread of night,
half the village set alight.
Then next day finding your head teacher
protecting the school from this fearful creature,
flameproofing the roof, soundproofing the doors
to block out the noise of its dragony roars.
While you're inside, preparing for SATS,
the dragon is feasting on barbecued cats.
Avoiding the dragon will drive you insane.
I suggest you rename your path, 'Sweet Hamster Lane.'

THE CELTIC CAT

(I don't know if there is any connection between cats and dragons in Celtic mythology – I suspect not. But it would be interesting if there were.)

The Celtic Cat is familiar with dragons,
It knows their secrets, has visited their lairs.
It has admired itself in the mirrored shields
of dragons' treasure troves.
It has singed its tail and whiskers
in the heat of their fire.

The Celtic cat travels to the places
where dragons gather. It would willingly
surrender the lives it has
for an offer of eternity.
And yet, there is already much of the dragon
in the cat itself – a hologram of flame
in its eyes, claws that could rip a hole
in the fabric of our world, through which
myths and memories pour out.

The Celtic cat understands that once,
dragons knew everything –
it desires that knowledge for itself.
A dragon's tongue, a dragon's teeth, a dragon's heart,
soon they will belong to the Celtic cat,
and the cherished secret of flight revealed
from the deepest wells of a dragon's soul.
For this is its birthright, its destiny,
cat and dragon, one and the same,
eyes, wings, dragon flame . . .

A WATERFALL OF
POSSIBILITIES...

WHERE DREAMS BEGIN

Everybody's always looking for
that place where dreams end,
but I'm looking out for the place
where dreams begin.

I'm looking for that starting point
where the excitement unravels,
the point where ideas interlink
and travel, tumbling down
from the brain in a waterfall
of possibilities.

That's the place where I like to be,
the place where nothing
has yet been attempted
and it's a long journey
before anything goes wrong.

It's that place where I'm not tied
to earth any more,
I can let my dreams rise.
Let them soar like a kite
that easily takes flight

And there's nothing to weigh
me down, no warning sound
to hold me back. It's a blank canvas
to which I can pin anything.

Yes, I'm looking for that place
where dreams begin,
I'm looking for my path to the sky.

AN ARTIST'S TOUCH

'We must not be ambitious. We cannot aspire to masterpieces. We may content ourselves with a joyride in a paintbox.' (Winston Churchill, former British Prime Minister)

Let's mix red and green and gold,
let's work with bold colours
and not be shy.
Let's tip up colours till the mix is right,
let's darken the day and lighten the night.

Let's blow bubbles with the blue,
spread fire with the red.
Let's green up grey places
and add yellow to the gloomiest corner.

Let's splash into white
and sky dive purple.
Let's drive on tracks of black.
Let's dance into a sunset glow.

Let's travel on paper to icy wastes,
to desert sands, and vibrant jungles.
Let's create oceans with a wipe of a brush,
a gush of white, a spill of blue.

Let the colours merge, let them flow
into a rainbow of shades
that only we know.

Let's find colours
that no one has found before.

On our joyride in a paintbox,
let's explore . . .

THE FRIENDSHIP BENCH

Every colour
and every creed,
People with money
and people in need.
We want
everyone sitting on the friendship bench.

Football fans
from rival teams.
'Beat you next time.'
'In your dreams.'

We want mums and dads
who can't get along,
brothers and sisters
always in the wrong.
We want
everyone sitting on the friendship bench.

We want families crying,
squabbling, bickering,
noisy neighbours
tempers quickening.

Overloud voices
sounding out,
pressure groups shouting
what they're about,
everyone sitting on the friendship bench.

We want criminals, judges,
prisoners and jailers,
bullies and victims,
thieves, blackmailers,
everyone sitting on the friendship bench.

No need to argue,
no need to fight,
nobody thinking that
might is right,
just
everyone sitting on the friendship bench.

We want positive, negative,
black and white,
darkness giving way
to the light.

We want hope for the future,
lessons from the past,
the sort of friendship
that lasts and lasts.
We want
everyone sitting on the friendship bench.

We want aggravation,
assimilation,
recrimination,
United Nations,
everyone sitting on the friendship bench.

From the naughty corner
to the friendship bench,

everyone sitting on the friendship bench,
everyone sitting on the friendship bench,
everyone sitting on the friendship bench.

So go on, say who
you'd like to see,
on the friendship bench
sitting peacefully
with you
and
me.

DAYS

Days fly by on holidays,
they escape like birds
released from cages.
What a shame you can't buy
tokens of time, save them up
and lengthen the good days,
or maybe you could tear out time
from days that drag, then pay it back
on holidays, wild days,
days you wish would last forever.
You could wear these days with pride,
fasten them like poppies to your coat,
or keep them in a tin, like sweets,
a confection of days
to be held on the tongue
and tasted, now and then.

ENTERING A CASTLE

Don't enter a castle quietly
    or timidly.
Don't enter it anxiously,
    ready to bolt
    at the slightest sound.
Don't enter it stealthily
    taking slow and thoughtful steps,
    considering with each footfall
    the mystery of history.
Don't be meek
    or frightened to speak.
For when you enter a castle
    you should *charge* through the gate
    and signal your arrival with a **SHOUT!**
You should play the invading army
    and **barge** a way through.
You should *swagger* up to the door
    then **shove** it aside and announce,
    'Here I am! This is mine!'

This castle is here, it is waiting for you,
    and today,
        it is yours for the taking!

DECEMBER MOON

The moon has come out too soon,
it's still the middle of the afternoon
and the day shows no sign of darkness.

What is the moon doing,
sneaking into the sky when it's light?

What is the moon playing at?
Couldn't it sleep?
Has its alarm clock rung too soon?

Do we see the moon this early
in June or September?

Or does December bring a special moon,
a let's-get-these-nights-over-soon moon,
a can't-wait-for-Christmas-to-come moon?

TIME

Time is like a thread that unwinds through our lives,
tight here, a bit of slack there.
Some people say they have too much time,
and that time hangs heavy.
I wish I could take some of theirs,
I never have enough time.
It would be great too, if I could summon up time
from some time in the future,
grab a bit from when I'm older,
cut it out and say, 'Look, I'll have it now,
I can use it, I've got plenty to do with it.'
Or wouldn't it be great to have a computer bank
of stored time, a nationwide time bank
you'd just need a pin to access,
to pay in or take out of . . .
Today's boring so I'd like to pay in three hours,
take it out again at the weekend
to stretch a day at Alton Towers.
That's how I felt when I was a child.
But now I'm older, I think I might regret
all that time I took so eagerly,
spending it recklessly, wastefully,
letting it slip through my fingers,
thinking it was only time,
that there would always be plenty more,
but there's not . . .

ZZZZZEDS

How much more
could I have done with my life
if I hadn't needed
so many zzzzzeds?
My shopping done
in all night supermarkets,
all the films
I could have seen,
books I could have read
instead of zzzzzeds,
instead of sleeping away
one-third of my life,
that precious stuff,
short enough as it is.
I could have learned languages,
Serbo-Croat or Japanese,
easy if you don't need sleep.
I could have studied more,
trained hard to be a doctor,
or a fighter pilot.
I could have travelled to places
I never dreamt I'd visit,
if I hadn't needed
so many zzzzzeds.
If I'd filled my head with actions
rather than dreams.

All the schemes, scams,
I could have masterminded,
the quiz programmes I could have
worked at to win.

So tonight I'm going to stay awake,
I'm just not going to sleep,
I'm just not going to sl . . . zzzzzzzzzzzzzz.

ABOUT THE AUTHOR

Brian Moses has been a professional children's poet since 1988. To date he has had over 200 books published, including volumes of his own poetry such as *A Cat Called Elvis* and *Behind the Staffroom Door* (both Macmillan), anthologies such as *The Secret Lives of Teachers* and *Aliens Stole My Underpants* (both Macmillan) and picture books such as *Beetle in the Bathroom* and *Trouble at the Dinosaur Cafe* (both Puffin).

Over 1 million copies of Brian's poetry books have now been sold by Macmillan.

Brian also runs writing workshops and performs his own poetry and percussion shows. To date he has given over 3,000 performances in schools, libraries, theatres and at festivals throughout the UK and abroad. He has

made several appearances at the Edinburgh Festival, been writer-in-residence at Castle Cornet on Guernsey and at RAF schools in Cyprus. Recently he has visited several international schools in Germany, Switzerland, Belgium, Italy, Spain, France, Iceland and Ireland.

CBBC commissioned him to write a poem

for the Queen's eightieth birthday and he was invited by Prince Charles to speak at his Cambridge University summer school in 2007.

He is also founder and co-director of a national scheme for able writers administered by his booking agency, Authors Abroad.

'Days' and 'Aliens Stole My Underpants' were both included in the BBC book *The Nation's Favourite Children's Poems*. 'Walking with My Iguana' was the most listened-to poem on the Poetry Archive for much of 2015.

For more information, go to:
www.brianmoses.co.uk
brian-moses.blogspot.com
www.poetryarchive.org

ABOUT THE ILLUSTRATOR

Raised by wild guinea pigs in the jungles of West Yorkshire, Chris Garbutt developed the uncanny ability to emit funny pictures with his mind. He now works out of a giant blue airship hovering two miles above central London and only ever comes to the earth's surface to buy cakes.